DEATH AT CAMP PAHOKA

Also by F. Richard Thomas

Poetry
Frog Praises Night: Poems with Commentary
Alive with You This Day
Corolla, Stamen, and Style
Fat Grass
Heart Climbing Stairs
Miracles
The Whole Mustery of the Bregn

Fiction
Prism: The Journal of John Fish

Nonfiction
Literary Admirers of Alfred Stieglitz

Editor
*Americans in Denmark: Comparisons of the Two Cultures
by Writers, Artists, and Teachers*
The Landlocked Heart: Poems from Indiana
Centering Magazine
Years Press Chapbooks

DEATH AT CAMP PAHOKA

poems by

F. Richard Thomas

Michigan State University Press
East Lansing

∞The paper used in this publication meets the minimum requirements of ANSI/NISO Z39.48–1992 (R 1997) (Permanence of Paper).

Michigan State University Press
East Lansing, Michigan 48823-5202

05 04 03 02 01 00   1 2 3 4 5 6

Library of Congress Cataloging-in-Publication Data

Thomas, F. Richard.
    Death at Camp Pahoka : poems / by F. Richard Thomas.
        p. cm.
    ISBN 0–87013–563–5 (alk. paper)
    I. Title.
    PS3570.H5626 D4 2000.
    811'.54—dc21

                                                                00–009530

Book and cover design by Michael J. Brooks

Visit Michigan State University Press on the World Wide Web at:
www.msu.edu/unit/msupress

For Sherry, Severn, and Caeri

Contents

5. *Don't wait, come home*

6. *To make us whole*

7. *All the wondrous mysteries*

Acknowledgments

The author gratefully acknowledges the following publishers, publications, and their editors, where poems in *Death at Camp Pahoka* originally appeared, often in earlier versions: *The Albany Review, The Bridge, The Burning World, California State Poetry Quarterly,* Canoe Press *(Miracles, 1996), Elvis in a Box, Driftwood Review, English Journal, Fear of Women, Green River Review, Images,* Lake Shore Publishing, *Light Year '88, Lunium Wonders, The Michigan Reading Journal,* The MacDowell Colony *Newsletter, Mobius, Nature Adores a Vacuum,* Odense University Engelsk Institut, *New Poems from the Third Coast* (Wayne State University Press), *Our Brown County, Potpourri,* The Raintree Press, The Red Cedar Writing Project Summer Institute, *Seedhouse: The Magazine for Modern Writers and Poets,* The Society for the Study of Midwestern Literature, *Strategies for Reading and Writing, Teacup, Writing Poetry* (B. Drake, Harcourt Brace Jovanovich); "Art in the Air," WPON-FM (Pontiac, Michigan) for a prize for the poem "Death at Camp Pahoka."

I appreciate the Michigan Council for the Arts grant and the cooperative support of the Department of American Thought and Language at Michigan State University that afforded me time away from the classroom to complete this book.

Although many people deserve thanks for reading and commenting on individual poems, I would like especially to acknowledge Alice Friman, Martha Bates, Roger Pfingston, Leonora Smith, and Sharon Thomas for their close readings of the entire manuscript. They not only helped me improve individual poems, but they provided invaluable suggestions for structuring the whole. Thanks also to Roger B. Smith for his expertise with the visual artwork.

1. Do not resist

Verge

This morning comes like Spain to my house:
suddenly the sun slashes
between the two houses across the field
and strikes through my kitchen window, across my table,
and into the sink.
The goldfish is stunned in the bowl.
On the orange crate
the odor of thick woods waits in the fern's leaves.
My pencil is suspended above clean paper.
The ocean has pushed out one bright drop that hangs
from the spigot.
I will move
when the fish moves.

New Geographies

Because I want to be ravished by new geographies,
I leap to the backs of cabooses
as they sway and clatter to shadow lands.
In this long bed that rumbles through the dark,
I follow the soft blue track in your neck
that curves over your collarbone,
between your breasts,
down the crease where muscles meet over the womb,
into the dream of light,
where I hurtle through barriers of breath and time
and everything is new and clean again.

What Opens

"When the sperm cells obediently arrive in the vicinity of the calling egg . . . molecules on the egg's surface may cast out a kind of fishing line, hook the sperm, and reel it in."

Shadows of Forgotten Ancestors, Sagan and Druyan (309)

When you arrive at the pinnacle of a mountain in Spain
that overlooks the Mediterranean,
you tremble, where the air is thin;
your heart knocks in your throat like Death
and long fingers of wind
dance down the mountains from Granada,
ruffle the hair on the back of the head,
caress the ancient terraces,
lift the hem of the sea's silk dress,
and you have no choice:
a door opens to Yes,
a tongue from the far side hooks you,
reels you in.
You enter—undone, transformed, possessed.

Before the closed door, when the bolt slips in the catch,
when the hinge sighs,
and a sudden inspiration,

　　　　　　　　　　like a soft gasp,

greets you at the threshold,
do not resist.
Pass over.

2. Fingers, lips

On Finding A Dusty Copy
Of Tropic of Cancer
At the Back of My Bookshelf

Musk and Turkish tobacco
pack my throat and lungs,
lump in my stomach,
and I feel the old ache
for the seedy and sweaty.
From the body's damp hollows
pungent roses sprout.
I would eat them,
swallow them to their roots in the skin's loam,
suck the goat-smell of death
and come alive,
musk and smoke
hissing and moaning like waves
through the dark blood
in my veins.

Popping in Hot Ghee

Some things are better in the mind
than in the flesh.
Wagner's *Tristan and Isolde* for example
is almost as good as sex.
But the odor of mustard seeds popping in hot ghee
is better than both, unless, of course,
you can do them all, all together;
then you approach something like religion,
something like Santa Barbara, California,
which is better if you've never been there
(so I've been told!);
or something like the taste of Retsina in a copper cup
in Plaka in Athens, which,
on the other hand,
you really ought to do
(I would imagine);
or even better yet,
something like smelling *Tristan and Isolde*
in the palms of your hands
after feasting on vermicelli
nestled in garlic, basil, olive oil, and piñones.
Now, that, I know you've got to experience.
In the flesh, that is.
I think.
I don't know.
Maybe I'm confused.
Let's fuck anyway.

After Shower and Shave

Tonight
the young mother next door
leaves the shade up
while she undresses for bed.
Watching her
from your dark room,
your ears tingle against your hair,
the boards beneath the carpet squeak,
and you think for a moment
the cat's moan
is a wheezing in your lungs
or your wife calling
from the kitchen below;
and when she swings her eyes
across your window,
you drop to all fours,
the towel sliding from your waist,
a flake of perfumed toilet paper and blood
falling from your silken jaw,
your heart hammering,
your hands and knees on fire
against the floor.

Fingers, Lips

"Always the procreant urge of the world."
Walt Whitman

Rose.
Orchid.
Rhododendron.
Anemone petals.
Hyacinth antennae.
Honeysuckle nectar.
Clematis pistil cilia.
Nasturtium, Wisteria, and Trillium.
Carpel, androecium, corolla, stamen, and style.
Beyond all reason.

After Knee Surgery

I wake from codeine dreams
and feel a smooth leg against my inner thigh.
How wonderful, I think,
that even St. Mary's condones a conjugal visit;
or better yet,
perhaps some new nurse-patient post-knife therapy.
But when I turn to put my arm around a waist,
there's no one there.
And when I lay my hand upon the disembodied thigh,
I find it's me,
my prepped and sexy hairless leg I've fallen for.
Suddenly I understand tranvestites, transexuals, lesbians.
To make love to a hairy man
must be like squirming in wool pants
                        in a hot and sticky church pew.
I gave up religion for that reason.
Must I now relinquish manhood, too?
O surgeon, woolly satan,
bring back the knife and prep me head to toe!
I want to love me everywhere!

After Sin, Penitence

They are like sacraments,
these Indian chutneys:
        mango, herb, and tomato;
and, O, these pickles:
        lemon, aubergine, green, and prawn!
Recipes thousands of years in the making,
imported for my pleasure,
they tease my lips and tongue,
warm my chest,
sit like the sun in my belly, till I'm dancing on fire,
my forehead glowing,
radiating the spirit of Vishnu and Shiva.
        But, O, mild Jesus,
where are you?
Come fold me in your arms.
Let me confess this proud excess!
I recant the pickles, the peppers, my intemperate taste!
O give me penance to make me chaste.
But please don't take my Vindaloo Paste!

3. And the night goes dumb

Shadows Fleeing

I swear
in some old places, some ancient towns,
like Bentheim, Rothenburg, Caerllion, or Rhyl,
people just vanish into thin air.
I've seen them turn the corner and be gone,
leaving roses and cobblestones,
lovers and loved,
behind.
I don't expect that of you here,
in our home town,
on the street, say,
between the Campus Theater and Discount Records,
or the First National Bank and the Peanut Barrel.
So I take you for granted,
except when I see smoke,
or steam,
or trains,
shadows fleeing from the corners of my eyes,
or you.

Separation

Beery-eyed,
I flip the TV off and flop on the couch in the family room.
You're gone. The whole house knows.
I try to read a mystery—
a thing I said I had no time to do
before the kids grew up.
I hate mysteries. But I don't like beer either,
so I get another one, flop again on the couch,
pop the top and start to tip another swig when
I hear a noise in the yard.
I wobble from the couch, dislodge
the stick in the jamb, varoom
the glass door back . . .
        Nothing.
Slight breeze.
Comfortable suburban frogs.
Singing to each other.
Some neighbor's child thinks he plays Moon River
on the clarinet.
The apples are the moon's moons.
A tide of dew is breaking up the lawn.
If I turn around, I will want to see you home
in a smile of verbs and light.
        I press my numb nose against the screen,
close my eyes and croak at the frogs,
and the night goes dumb.

Midsummer Night

After work,
on the Interstate,
   I'm sure I see you in the opposite lane.

At home,
drowsy in my easy chair,
I wince when the sun cuts through the blinds
and into my eyes.

I dream I eat the rose,
                your final gift.
How beautiful we are and, by firelight, how fierce
before you disappear.

Laying my hand on the phone,
I feel your hand on your phone, too.

I touch my fingers to my throat
where velvet petals claw.

   Eyes closed,
I float in blood and fire.

Divorcing

Your face has not shaped my hand for years.
And though our children are beautiful,
your eyes are dulled by pain and loss.
When you look at me,
your ghost turns and walks from the room.

This is the nightmare
in which we peer from separate worlds,
as through the membrane of a dream,
but only meet in glimpses.

I can't reach you.
In the morning,
hoping the new day will bring us home,
I try to turn to you,
but the birds
that died in my chest all yesterday
have littered our bed.

It's no dream.
I don't know you.

To think
that only thirty years ago,
one night I touched your face
and tiny galaxies
sparkled
between our skins.

All Aboard

In the sleeping car
our bodies interfold
like hands in prayer.

Early morning,
when the train chuffs to a stop,
you get off
and I don't know why.
There is no crowd, no clock, no name, no station.
But this is your stop.

When the train departs,
and we hiss and whistle away in widening circles,
        I see you suddenly clap your hands
then tap your toes;
and when tears come to your eyes,
you start to dance,
kicking your heels
till the sand stings your knees.

Even though I run from front to back and yell,
bruise my fists on the thick windows and doors,
this train won't stop again.

I watch you cry and dance
until you are a tiny dervish
under white clouds
that sit in the sky like boulders.

Something
I have not understood.

The next thing I know
you are gone for good.

Now That the World is Broken

No reason for the stiff limb to lift,
nor the brow,
nor heart, nor eye.

A tattered quilt,
the soul is
blown and whispered
to fitful wisps.

White, white
the tangled and broken whorl
of the mind in the dark.

Dark, dark
all thresholds,
passageways,
all useless destinations.

4. As if what it says it will say forever

Bailadora

When I was a boy,
I summited a small peak in Andalusia,
scrambled past the olive trees, the sheep, the silent shepherd
who turned his head away.
At the top,
waves of mountains rolled over my shoulder to Granada,
and before me
the Mediterranean shined all the way to Africa
       like a vast upturned bell of resin
       in which specks of dolphin leapt like sperm.
The whole wind swept through me like a *bailadora de flamenco*.
I sang and wept and returned to the village
with a mountain in my chest.

Now, as a man,
when I lie beneath the gypsy stars,
dolphins swim with me,
sleep with one eye open to keep me from drowning—
the weight of it,
the mountain, lying down with me:
ballast for the voyage home.

Still Life, Summer Night

In a white room
you write on the ivory table,
where peaches, plums, and nectarines
blaze in a silver dish.
Liter of Beaujolais.
Dark blood cork twisted
on the gleaming screw.
Black lamp, dropped from the ceiling,
holds you in an egg of light.

Barefoot, lotus,
in lime gauze dress,
you perch on your stool like Shiva.
Your thumb, forefinger
massage your brown breastbone,
revealing pale skin
where the sun could not touch.
Black pencil
tight between your teeth.

In a dark corner
I crouch on the leather saddle chair.
I pretend not to watch.

You pour wine.
It guggles and pearls into the crystal tulip.

You slip the pencil from your teeth
and write a word
and stop.

You reach for a nectarine.

Your teeth slide into the fruit.

Your lips are wet.

Outside in the warm dark
the sea is too quiet.

If I listen hard
I hear sand crabs
clicking from their holes.

I think the moon is standing still.

Paisano Wine

When we first married,
I thought we'd live the simple life,
drink Paisano wine from jelly jars, forever.
But when my back was turned,
we got two sets of dishes,
long-stemmed wine-glasses, a house with central air,
two kids complete with basketball goal over the garage door
and soccer balls behind the arborvitae.
And after thirty years,
we've even got this holiday in Spain,
where we sprawl asleep on silky sheets,
anesthetized by sun and drink
and unconcern for anything;
and where now the morning sun
pries through the window with a breeze
that frees the curtains from the wall,
clinks our champagne glasses together on the lampstand
and tickles my dangling foot.
I zip my hands and legs across the sheet
to slide the whole wide bed
and rest my head against your spine.
And there it is again,
something in your skin:
familiar smell along your shadowed back,
your shoulder blade, your gleaming shoulder, ear, and neck,
the hint, the trace,
pulsing at your sunburnt throat,
of ashes,
ashes.

San Miguel,
After Thirty Years

At the back of a dresser drawer
that smells of bleach, old leather,
stale perfume, and coins,
I find, neatly wrapped in yellow lined paper,
a photograph of you, my wife,
and hold it to the light.

San Miguel de Allende, 1963
Cigarros Faros   Cerveza Negra Modelo
Ham Tortas and Pineapple
Pulque Limones Tequila
Bells of the pink gothic *catedral*
Bougainvillea bursting from our patio roof.
Down Calle de la Canal,
cubes of stucco houses spill into the brown valley
where a steam train spits through blue mountains.
Night at Taboado springs—
my tongue on your neck,
lips on your hip and thigh,
your teeth skimming my shoulder and breast—
hot waters swirl diamonds
around our tight silken skin.
Mountain shadows drift and flow as the moon slips down,
pulls the gauze from savage stars.
At noon,
rains thunder, steam, wash cobblestones
slick and shining,
and pomegranates
bleed in our mouths all summer.

There is nothing to want,
my Guantanamera, nothing to want,
not with you on our new sarape in front of this fire,
nothing to want, Maleguena Salerosa, nothing.
Nothing more to want
when you are as you are in this photograph,
loving yourself in your skin,
loving who I am,
loving you,
snapping the shutter at the very heart
from which all Mexico radiates.
Nothing, the two of us, naked in San Miguel, your body
saying what we both know we want it to say,
as if what it says it will say forever.

O Donna

My wife contemplates her figure in the mirror,
puckers her dress correctly under her belt,
while I adjust my coat and shirt.
        But, Donna, I am thinking of you
pressed against me in my light blue Nash—
that glistening moonlit egg: fragrance of beer
sun lotion, motor oil, Chantilly,
and Herbert Tareytons.
Our song, Elvis, crackles on the radio.
I cut the headlights.
Your shoulder, your hip, your knee,
your cool leg against mine;
your very breathing stuns my breath away
as we bump, rumble, and sway
through the field and down the farmlane
to the secret beach on the Ohio River.
I don't want no other love.

In swimsuits
we posture on the sand.
White-edged clouds skim the stars
that hang above the silhouette of trees
a mile across the river in Kentucky.
Your straps have fallen to your elbows,
and the silver light that lies on your skin
seems to lift your face and arms away from your body.

Phantom silken hair
on your shoulders and neck and jaw
and over your dark lips shines.
Small waves flake into sequins,
gurgle and shush. Warm
ghosts of air
sigh the sweet musk of riverbank woods
and bottomland cornfields.
I dig my toes deep into the sand,
then turn to slide my hand
upon your waist . . .

Someone I never met
fathered your children,
someone who knows you so well
he doesn't see your hips grow,
cruel lines rivering your face and neck.
You will never be for him
what you are for me:
translucent moment,
ethereal snapshot.
Yeah, Baby, it's still you I'm thinking of:
mirage,
shimmering through my life.

Ontogeny, Phylogeny, Opposable Thumb

Eating Sunday dinner with my family,
my bony thumb hangs over the plate's rim
next to its twin,
a chicken wing.
My mind will not resist:
      Fried,
would it taste the same?
Would the fat be buttery under the crisp, blistered skin?
Would the salty, sizzled blood complement
the sweet marrow?
I blanch and fret.

When my 4-year-old daughter says to pass the gravy,
she also asks me why I'm acting funny.
But I don't tell her of these obscenities:
the unruly similes and phobias
my mind conjures and forks forth,
even at Sunday dinner.
Instead I say, "Oh, I just bit my tongue,"
      and then I remember
the ashy taste of darkness in my mouth
when I could not sleep as a young child,
remember trying to cough the panic from my lungs
when lint and pillow feathers
whispered beneath my bed like flames.

As my daughter wields her knife and fork,
nimbler now with every passing day,
I glance sidelong at her face.
Her brow is ruined.
I know she knows:
she's on her own, alone,
her eyes ignited by imagination
and terror.

Goal

I will not pace the sidelines
to watch you scrap with the ball at your feet,
spin around a challenger, and,
staring into the goalkeeper's eyes,
slide the ball into the left hand corner.

Today
I will lean upon my computer,
daydream your victories,
and relish my good fortune:
to know that you are striving like an artist
to perfect your lively craft.
But if for lack of luck or concentration
you fail today,
your loss will still be less than mine:
my staying home, missing the chance
to watch you *be* my daughter.

But I will stay home:
to practice for the time when I can't live your life,
a time I'll need the skills to live my own,
confront your absence,
contemplate my blurry face in the blank screen,
and try to stumble on a goal.

Cosmetic

In the mirror
I push my hair away from my forehead,
pull my beard away from my jaw,
see my father
and laugh;
and when my brows arch
and wrinkles furrow my face
and corners of my eyes
and I see you, father, again,
I laugh again,
silently,
except for a kind of wheeze,
which I then remember as yours,
and so I laugh again,
just as you would have laughed,
and again,
      until I am beside myself with you.

             O dead father.
O funny dead father.

Presence

This afternoon
as I walked to Fire Pond,
suddenly,
from behind the trees,
moaning with the deep choir of wind in the pines,
the monstrous stones
like prehistoric leviathans
began to rise against me.
I stopped,
closed my eyes to calm the thrumming in my chest,
then confronted the path again,
the stones shifting imperceptibly as I passed.
There is no need to run.
There is no escape.

5. Don't wait, come home

Thirteen Years Old

After church
and Sunday dinner at the Merry-Go-Round,
where they smiled and greeted friends
     as well as those who trespassed against them,
he and his sister, mother, and father
sometimes went to the Washington Theater.
And when the Korean War came on Warner-Pathé,
when he saw the young soldiers, wounded,
brave, waving, or dead,
when he heard the newscaster's sure and righteous voice
riding a Sousa march,
he ran from the flickering dark
through padded doors
onto the bright green carpet,
then walked preposterously adult
through the deserted lobby
past the uniformed concession girl,
sneering and smacking gum,
painting the moons of her nails behind the corn popper,
past the Doublemint, Neccos, and Black Crows,
then flew up the curved stairway,
grasping the brass rail to pull him up
two steps at a time to the empty Gentlemen's Room:
small black and green tiles, odor of moth balls,
urine and wet cigarette butts.

At the urinal,
he leaned against the chrome flush-bar,
        cold as a gun against his forehead,
and thought,
If I only had Faith,
I could step over the edge,
walk on the rushing water,
away.

Excerpts from a Letter

(for my son, leaving home)

Dear Son:

In the late 40s, on muggy days before air-conditioning,
after fort-building or pretending the glories of war,
creases of dirt in my sweaty neck,
the key to the back door and my father's dog tags
dangling on a loose string against my chest,
I sat in the shade of the silver maple,
read Captain Marvel, Spiderman, or Phantom,
sipped water from my canteen, dreamed.
A DC-3 droned in the sun . . . .

In summer storms
rain sprayed through the porch screens onto my face,
arms, and hands, and a close, sudden flash and boom of thunder
buckled my knees;
then I shivered with joy and like a miracle the street was a river
for makeshift boats—destroyers and aircraft carriers—
and water fights.

Hot nights, after tincannio, red rover, and baths,
we sat on the front porch in the glider and metal lawn chairs
near the crickets and frogs
and the moths pipping against the screens.
We pitted cherries, snapped beans,
ate chocolate marshmallow ice cream, talked . . . .

I think we talked.
On a moonless night
Dad's cigarette glowed from his chair in the dark
corner of the porch—just clear of the street lamp's glare
that sometimes teared his shrapnel eye.
Some nights he didn't speak.
Bill Stern reported the sports.
My sister and I listened slack-jawed through Inner Sanctum
and competed to polish the shiniest apple in the world
on our pyjamas.
Mom rubbed our backs.
Sometimes we got to have a glass of Grandpa's peach wine.
Sometimes we got to sleep on the porch
next to the immense breath of the night . . .

Every night I fell asleep to trains
that chuffed and groaned in the switchyard miles away.
In late autumn, before my windows were closed against the cold,
the engines seemed so near.
Before I slept, I thought about the trains, about the edge of town,
about what lay beyond, in the country, beyond the country,
beyond Ditney Hills or even my grandparents' farm.

Someplace far, far beyond, even on the other side of war
and the magical terror of moonless nights,
I dreamed of something loosening,
as if the dark red lip and wet tongue of the apple
were unfolding, as if I could steal the golden mystery
of fire and peach wine and the secret musk
of the black cherries that stained my fingers . . . .

Recently, my son, I dreamed
of a key on a string that opens everything.
I wanted to raise it from my neck, lift it over my head.
I wanted to give it to you.

The Last Cherry Bomb

At the backyard party,
after blossoming of sparklers,
after bottle rockets burned bright pistils into the stars
and darkness flowed over us again like the sure course of blood
to the heart,
I prepared a grand Independence Day finalé:
I'd blow the seams of a 30 gallon garbage can,
blast the lid off in a mushroom of smoke,
frighten the unsuspecting kids,
and deafen the other adults into a stupor of memory—
the America that used to be,
when M-80's and cherry bombs were more fun than dangerous.

Oh, sure, as kids,
we'd heard of fireworks at the ballpark gone awry,
but only parents knew someone who lost an eye, perhaps,
or several fingers on the fourth of July.
Not someone we ever knew.
No.
This year, I'd take us back
to see if we could savor what we lost.

So I lit the 30-year-old sand-textured bomb and ran and waited.
But all we got was a flat fup and a small white puff.
My gallery burst the silence with their laughs,
squeaked back and forth in aluminum lawnchairs,
chortled and guffawed,
Their kids looked at each other, raised their eyebrows,
wondered what was funny to their crazed agéd parents.

Then I laughed, too—
laughed
at this failure of violence
in the backyard of our treelined street in our small town
where city lights had only slightly dimmed the stars,
and chirp and creak of tree frogs and crickets
rolled over us like fog
or sparkler smoke,
while much of the cherry-bombless-world beyond,
a fiction we barely understood,
roiled like an aneurysm
in the deep arteries of the night.

Dominatrix of Fleas

Fleas are guided by the smell of blood in the breath of the flea-handler.

Huddling shoulder to shoulder around the ring,
we flinch in unison
when the masked flea-handler cracks her whip
then exhales across the tiny tightrope, thin as a spider's web:

a miniature Dracula, cloaked in tiny black cape,
leaps a hand's length to the other side.

Dominatrix in black leather tights and bra,
she lures her fleas and mesmerizes us as well.

We misunderstood: this is no two-bit sideshow,
but vampires, sex, and plague.

We wonder if we have the nerve to leave,
the will to disobey her whip, her tights,
her white neck, her flesh.

Her heavy breath that holds her microscopic slaves in thrall
blows hot on our own faces now,
makes me wince.

I keep a wary eye on her,
the other on the leaping fleas,
then feel hard shoulders press into my arms.

I wonder, did I hear a snarl or moan?
I glance around to see if lips
are curling back from someone's teeth,

here, in the arena where I find myself with strangers,
dangerously bound
in the bloodlust circus tent.

2023rd Psalm

The Hoover's the sweeper I really want.

It maketh me to lie down with clean ashtrays.
It leadeth me to like sterile quarters.

It abhoreth my soil. It leadeth me down the paths
of cleanliness for its name's sake.

Yea. Though I walk through a hallway of filth
I will not feel queasy: for thou art with me;
thy wand and thy crevice tool they comfort me.

Thou preparest a sanitary place for me to feel good
in the presence of company.
(But thou annointest my head with turmoil
when thy bag runneth over.)

Surely Kirby, Bissel, Eureka, and Electrolux
are good enough,
but I want the brand I will follow
all the days of my life,
so I will dwell in the house of the Hoover for ever.

Night Train

"'Armageddon' in the lounge car in ten minutes."
(Announcement on the loudspeaker of the Empire Builder.)

Because it's the end of the millennium,
we're happy it hasn't spread beyond the lounge car.

But later, rocking back and forth in the top bunk
of our narrow roomette,
I realize, it *has*.

It started in the Alps, some thirty years ago:
A steam train drew a thin line down the valley
as we romped in an icy stream.
The water whirled around our aching ankles
and we dared each other to endure the pain.
Do you remember, there, the chestnut tree,
where you unwound your extravagant hair
and we lay naked as olive blossoms in spring?
How a sudden breeze thrilled our skin?
How we pulled bread and wine,
books and paper from our packs
and danced with our eyes
and the whole world danced along?

Then something happened,
inconspicuously and without prophecy.

And now, as I'm tossed to sleep in this sleek train
that cleaves through the night,
I dream of our home in Illinois,
where we turn and turn in the separate pods of our bed—
the clean and cozy coffin
from which we groan and rise from fitful sleep
to greet the lethal business that metastasizes through our days:
clackety-clack, clackety-clack.

Urban Flight

Trying to flee the irritating city,
you find you are trapped in traffic
on the Beltway in your BMW,
breathing hard,
heart racing,
suddenly not sure you have a wife and children
who will remember and love you if you return.
You're not even sure
that you are driving to some destination,
or that you have a home.
Your ulcer's acting up.
Perhaps the loss of blood already heaves you into dreams.

If you survive,
if you arrive at the place you call home—
a place where people seem to be your kin,
barely changed from when you saw them last,
still slightly smiling when you enter,
but your wife's nose too tipped and haughty,
her usually perfect lipstick slightly skewed,
her cowlick missed by the curling iron,
your son and daughter sullen, distant, almost rude—
what will you do?

What can calm
the hums and cries and murmurs as you shower in the morning
or toss to sleep at night?
What will ease the ache that slithers 'round your house,
your lawn, beneath the seats in your car?
Is there nothing left to do?
Too late to stop,
and start anew,
to ask forgiveness and forgive,
begin to make a way to live?

Waiting Room

It isn't so much that it's Upper Sandusky.
It's that I'm two days on the road
and on my way home to Bloomington
when something starts thumping in the car
and I know I'll be on the shoulder waiting for a tow truck
if I don't get off I-75 and head for the Ford garage.

And that's where I am, in the Waiting Room,
    where two toddlers screech and whine,
        and bang each other on the shoulders with their elbows.
Their anorexic mother in western boots, platinum hair,
                      and tight jeans,
                smacks the boy across the lips
          then mashes her Marlboro into the ashtray.
A balding stump of a woman in a coat with no buttons
                   knits a sock and sighs,
while the skinny highschool dropout
            with missing tooth and Auto-Lite Cap
      slices the grease from his fingernails with a pocketknife
                  and jerks his head.
A smart businessman fidgets in the doorway,
He's watching TV and jangling his keys.
His neck puffs over the tight collar of his shirt and tie.

It's summer and hot, too, in this tiny waiting room,
                 and I can't think straight,
   and I wonder if I should eat my soft and blotchy day-old peach.

Through the thin wall
I hear the rattling shriek of air wrenches,
                    but I wonder if they're working on *my* car.
It's taking so long and the waiting room TV is so loud.

    It's a soap opera on the TV and a beautiful couple
    kiss and paw each other's neck and face and ears and
    their hair's getting mussed
    and I do not believe they are from Ohio
    and then in the next scene
    the same man is arguing with his wife, a different woman,
        about their kids. She points her finger at him
and this is obviously their second or third or fourth marriage

        and who knows who is the father of these kids
    or if they're their kids, or if the real father's dead
    or if he's maybe waiting in some greasy Ford garage,
waiting for his car to be fixed and daydreaming
about his former wife,
or his present wife, or even his only wife and their children
    who become more and more beautiful
        as he waits
        and waits.

Somehow I've got to do things differently.
    This heat and smell of grease and sweat,
the young toothless man, the sad children,
the frightened mother, the bald woman, the jangling keys,
the cinched neck, the TV, this Ford garage:

It's my life.
It's a hole in my stomach.
It's whatever it is that says,
"You've got to do something besides get up in the morning
to eat and drive and toil and buy and drink and sleep.
You've got to love your kids and wife,
you've got to get out of Upper Sandusky and make love,
you've got to love your life,
send up a fire balloon, learn to work and dance again.
You've got to try to touch God's finger.
Your body's fine,
                your mind's OK,
                        everybody's here,
        the peach you eat perfumes your neck and palms.
Don't wait,
                come home."

6. To make us whole

Annual Family Slide Show

The snapshot of you sprawled on your bed,
mouth gaping, three years old and dead-asleep
in your blue Danish slicker and rain hat,
always makes us laugh.

For a moment
I think a bead of water
slides down the grey window behind you.

How many years ago I struggled up two flights
to lay you there.

I wonder:
one day
when you clasp your own child in your arms,
will you remember
fingers curled over your shoulder,
palm on the back,
thumb in the damp hair at the base of the skull,
heart climbing stairs with you?

Daughter/TV/Spring

Awakened by voices in the house,
I find you asleep on the couch
under the TV's babble and glare.
One arm dangles on the floor;
your jaw is slack; mouth open;
a trickle of saliva from pale lips.

When I switch it off, you turn to the wall.
In the gray face of the screen
we are two cells smeared between glass.
I sit beside you on the couch,

and the window shade swells, scrapes on the sill,
plops, billows again,
as a green breath of soil and wet grass
sighs through the window.
Chickadees and robins chirrup and cheer.
Hint of wood-ash drifts from the hearth,
and outside the picture window
the pink blossoms of the cherry tree stipple
the amber glow of dawn.

I comb my fingers through your hair;
the musk of lilacs rises behind my eyes like a hymn;
your moist temple flowers in a pulse
against my palm.

Entomology

Approximately 35 species of microscopic creatures that number
the human population of the earth live on every human body.

His father's gray leg, flecked with limp and black scraggly hairs,
lay like a stain on the sheets.
The entomologist hefted his father's calf in his hand,
as if he were cradling an egg.
Once hard and square,
it hung now like a pouch of webworms.
And within his father's dying skin, arthropods—a world
of imperceptible arachnids, insects, and myriapods—
different species with tusks and claws, antennae and
polypositional mandibles.

As oxygen receded from his father's extremities—the far
reaches of the heart's galaxy—the entomologist saw in the
mottled skin—the purpling patches on the legs—grand
banquets, joyous feasts for the invisible parasites.
He believed that he felt them on his own body—the vague
itch here, the irritation there—the gnawing of tiny carnivores.
He knew they were under the bed, too—dust mites—waiting
beneath couches and chairs for the miraculous rain of
manna, flakes of dead flesh.

Returning from his reverie the entomologist found himself
bending to his father's smile, where he overheard first
an ethereal whisper, then a long sigh,
"Take, eat; this is my body, given for the biosphere.
This do in remembrance of me."
Then it was finished.

Glancing at his daughter, he knew she had not heard
and would not know what she heard if she had.
She swung her young, sturdy legs in the green
Naugahyde chair in a white corner
of a nursing home in the universe.
Outside the window in the branches of the juniper,
he saw a flock of Cedar Waxwings dart and flit,
pluck red berries,
then depart like a sudden exhalation,
to set an Argiope spider's golden web dancing
in the October sun.

Soccer Match

(For the Michigan Hawks, USYSA Women's U-19 National
Championship Team, 1989.)

Today, my daughter, you let the ball
fall from an arc
twice as high as our house,
slide down your right thigh,
knee, the birthmark on your calf,
ankle, the bruise on your heel,
and spurt into the open grass,
the space toward which you had already moved,
then somehow touched it once again
to place it right before the left wing's foot
some forty yards away.

I don't know how you did this.
But, then, I marvel at my own walking,
tying my shoes,
lifting a cup to my lips
and setting it down,
clicking the radio on and off.

I think I see what this means:

the miracles we are.
And how miraculous
to be miracles
together.

Reunion: A Love Poem

This is not
about the way we navigate the day.
Not about dropping off the drycleaning.
Not about the traffic on the freeway,
nor bending over desks,
pushing paper, pencils, punching keys,
making calls,
rubbing aching eyes before our blurry monitors.
This is not about the way
we buy our beer and pantyhose,
then stop for milk and bread,
then haul our slumped and lumbering bodies home
to grunt through dinner, nod through news,
fidget over daughter's freshman algebra,
palpitate when son decides to play his violin;
nor litigating children's bedtime hour.

No,
this is
touching you
in the dark of our room,
the nudge and snuggle of my hand
up under your breast.
This is
sending my soul out travelling
along the streams and currents of my arm
to come to rest,

come to breathe in slowly, peacefully,
and ease into your warmth,
sleep blissfully,
yes,
finally,
at home
within your sure and pillowed
woman's midnight hollows.

Slow Dancing at the Med-Inn

It's the night before your mastectomies.

I'm sitting on the end of the bed.

(We got the faded-orange-curtain-40-watt-lightbulb-
green-chenille-bedspread room.)

From the shower,
you suddenly loom over me,
smelling of peppermint soap
and wet leaves around the lake in fall.

Holding a breast in each hand,
as if restraining the flight of doves,
you press them to my face and erupt into tears.

I touch my lips to one, then the other,
falter at the scent of myself—
the joyful signature of my fingers and hands.

I pull your body hard to mine,
as if to hurt will help to heal.

The room fades in and out like a bad radio.
The baseboard heater tick tick ticks.

Outside, the helicopter walloping on the roof
lowers a burned child,
stars explode across the night,
volcanoes rise from the ocean floor,
wobble the earth on its axis.

Except for our breathing,
we dare not move.

Wisdom

"Dead trees are transmuted into living animals and vice versa.
When you doubt the wisdom of this arrangement, take a look at
the prothonotary [warbler]."

Aldo Leopold, *A Sand County Almanac*

I will lose myself in the cheesy vernix
that swaths my newborn child
and in the purple splotches
that flower on my father's leg as he dies.
I will be lost in the smell of woods,
the infinity of crickets,
and the day the bamboo bloom.
I will give myself over to the irrepressible laugh
that seizes the body
and pulls it under, like orgasm, or sneeze.

I will not wonder what things mean.
I shall give up religion and philosophy.

For a moment,
I will be the warbler, gold and blue—
perfume exhaled from decaying trees,
as if life and death were a seamless breeze.

Ascension

(for our 33rd Anniversary)

Alone
I am no equal
to the floating lotus,
the levitating meditator,
or Christ aloft.
But, O, the two of us!
When I regard your visionary eye,
your rising forehead,
the cathedral of your ear,
your arching thumb,
when I behold your pelvis and your collarbone
like wings, turn heavenward,
then I rise too,
with you:
together, twice as holy
in our muscular defiance of gravity
as any spiraling flower of God
or any saint in his lonely ascent.

The Gift

As family and in-laws gather around the tree on Christmas Eve,
you, my grown-up daughter, soon leaving home,
plop down on my lap and wreathe your arm around my neck,
as if you were just 12 or 10, or even 5 again.
Suddenly I recall your grace in the face of nature's chaos:
you skipped around the park, hugging,
kissing trees and rocks and bushes,
welcoming their roughness to your cheek;
even rubbing your palms over grass, as if to glean
some essence from the green.
But not until this moment do I learn what you intuited at five:
that matter holds the shape of spirit,
and matter's gift of love is sparked by touch—glance of eye,
music on the ear, flood of atoms on the nose and tongue,
whisper of flesh on the skin of a stone.

The pious say, in some far purer sphere,
uncluttered by the things we see and feel and hear,
we'll find our spirits in inseparable familial communion,
in bright and immaterial solution.

But I'll not hold my breath.
For now,
on the eve when even in-laws stay their fear of love,
you sit for a moment on my knee,
your arm circles my neck,
fingers dangle on my shirt;

and perhaps because it is for the last time,
your gesture gives me joy,
helps me understand what you already know:
we give ourselves away
to make us whole.

Joining Hands

I.
Predictably
I did not predict
the way the moonlight lifts your belly
into music.

This dream that we live
has a mind of its own.

II.
Often I think God does not matter.
While you sleep,
your diary spreads open over your heart.
Some words seep over your breasts
and trickle down your stomach.
This matters.

III.
When the red
split-leaf maple in the yard
blossoms in the iris of your opening eye,
I am astonished.

IV.
Suddenly,
in the middle of speechlessness,
we become moon and bone,
the language that should not be spoken
when we are like this,
silent and spacious poem.

V.

As the eagle's wings bewitch the wind's strength,
so our breathing becomes us.

VI.

As the diving eagle relinquishes the wind,
so our breathlessness becomes us.

VII.

Sometimes we lie together
as quietly as the grass.
Then how we love
to feel the wind running through us!

VIII.

No, it's not
the skin around our eyes
creasing deeper with age,
it's the light around our faces
becoming more intense,
as we move closer to the front of the stage,
joining hands for a bow.

IX.

We write
like we love,
as if,
in these bodies,
we could.

(Inspired by a reading of *The Essential Rumi,* trans. Coleman Barks.)

7. All the wondrous mysteries

Miracle

I get vertigo
walking the worn boards of old buildings,
and whirl like a one-winged bird
whenever I cock my head.

A sudden dull breeze rises in the crown of my skull,
eyes fall and fall, legs become slim twigs.
I am told that somewhere between ear and brain
neurons may be pressed, scrambled, starved, or dead.

But maybe I'm possessed by a presence
that would make me leave my feet,
swoop down, home in.
Or, like water witch or wizard,
perhaps I've got a gift for miracles;
perhaps appendages will sprout from my shoulder blades—
dark feathered things—
or new vision—
clear hawk's eyes—
to ease the turbulent flight.

And why not?

Birds don't fly because they have wings;

they have wings because they fly.

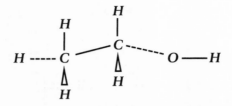

In a corner of your dark lab
the copper glow of lighted dials and gauges
effuses over bellies and elbows
of burettes, tubes, and bubbling stills.
With headphones clamped around your wiry hair,
you sway upon your stool, wagging your finger
to the atom sounds of ethanol,
the different tune the lone H plays
from H_5 in ensemble;
and you hear the whole compound,
the spirit of wine,
like alchemy,
become a polyvalent song,
sublime and quintessential symphony
to which the whole lab hums
in an ethereal psalm:
C_2H_5OH.

(For Francis Taulelle, chemist, who listens to the songs alcohol molecules make
when they boil off of molten salts.)

The Poet
and the
Japanese Particle Physicist

"Most particles or aggregates of particles that are ordinarily regarded
as separate objects have interacted at some time in the past with
other objects. The violation of separability seems to imply that in
some sense all of these objects constitute an indivisible whole."

Bernard d'Espagnat

In Cafe Luxembourg
under a warm lamp
that throws an egg of light around us,
you mix r's and l's
as naturally as the sun's rise and fall.
From you, I get light straight,
curved, that is,
relative to the mass it chances to pass
in its ethereal circuit.
Time, you show,
is not the worldly prison
(you say what sounds to me like "wordry plison")
we envision.

For fleeting hours,
mercurial time,
we sip our wine,
enchanted by the speed and quirks of light
and proton's life and quarks;
enchanted by the flowering of God:
by rhythms that bridge space and time,

81

webs that bind all subatomic particles,
devise a world or word,
and make this system we call "I" or "You"—
unfurling of the primordial explosion—
stand up
     and sing.

Egg

The egg in my hand: the center of the Universe.
Like the rose or newborn child,
it gathers space, makes it whole.
Like the drop of water on the kitchen spigot,
the egg is a shape God takes to intimate Her presence.

Dolphins, seals, and stones in streams
grow more like God each day.

At night in the city,
egg people glow as if the sun is in their bellies.
Walking by the orange aura from their apartment windows,
you hear flamenco,
the oval laughter, the lusty olé
of hearty men and women who conspire against the dark.
You will not forget the round clapping of their hands:
prayer and praise—an egg of noise the air makes
from a perfect joining of the palms.

In the country
egg people are mistaken for marsh gas, ghosts,
the moon on the pond, the eye of an owl.

The egg in my brain tap taps,
small beak in the dark.
I hold my breath, close my eyes, keep still,
hear the rip and tear
as the shell splits, and water flows—
death-defying images: ovum, seed, and womb,
sun trembling in the heart of the moon.

Returning the egg to its carton on the sill,
I see on the tree outside my window
in a soft breeze, dancing in the autumn rain,
red berries,
small flaming eggs in which the nebulae spin.

Artist's Demons

Because he cannot sketch them,
his heart, at the hearth, seeks the flames,
chaos that forges dreams—
his other life
as real in novelty and sequence as his days—
in which he sees but can't create the vision of desire.

Because his eye is dark and deep,
he knows no act of simple will
will help him sight the line his pencil makes;
he must let thought be gone,
let day be done,
and like an athlete lost in play
let dreams begin to draw themselves
to find and see integrity
of daemon
and divine.

Circumambulating Michelangelo's David

Circumambulating David,
I think I *will* my movement and my pace,
my pause,
my look,
    and pace again.

But then at night,
    in a dream,
I see that David *is* Michelangelo,
who watches my each move, and pace, and pause
and knows exactly where I'll pause
and look
    and pace
and look again.

What magic is this sleeping,
waking, slipping in and out of dreams?
What cosmic sleight-of-hand
makes us circle, wide-eyed, 'round realities
that circle us around?
What unseen sorcerer's fingers
slid the muscled stomach from the stone
to help us dream the light unleashed,
    the miracle,
        the common fire,
from which we birth,
and like the Michelangelos and angels,
rise to dance?

Butter

For boiled potatoes,
tender peas and toasted cheese;
on crackers with chili,
or soft-boiled eggs;
for sautéing salmon, garlic, or veal;
for lobster tails, or escargot;
nothing is better than butter.

When God created the world,
He said, "Let there be butter."
And He saw that it was good,
like man, ribs, woman,
holy water, and beer.

I believe in butter.
I buy my daily lot in ten pound tins,
simmer it on the stove as incense for the house.
After showers
I rub it on my elbows, knees, and hands,
use it to part my hair.
And, O, how great it is for sticky drawers
and making love.

But my clothes don't fit.
My wife and kids tell me to quit.
The doctor says I've got to stop.

During the day I feign cutting down,
but at night before I sleep,
I anoint my lips,
rub it under my nose and on my chest,
like Vicks,
put one glob in the center of my forehead,
and—buttered again—
know the Lord my soul will take
if I should die before I wake.

When I die,
I'll slide heavenward
on the golden greased pathway to God,
my body and soul
fat and slithery
with piety.

When We Dream

leathered men
ond handsome women,
ancient ond strong,
push away the cloads so the smah byrds
can come to syng the boatiful songs of the dead.
Ond then
we hear the scoiming of the byrds.
Thei thurt for song is greht,
as is thei toskk.
'Tis a greht foeit
for the tiny creaters
to foght sikd fullded, fragil wings
through sikd an jadrig hryff,
then byrst aouwt in a firry of music
into the whole mustery of the bregn
from wince they fly freely,
synging down the aerme
through the fingre,
through the pin
into the murthering light.

Writers

The northern lights danced on their faces
                          and silvered their eyes;
so they travelled to Kharkov and Cairo,
Lapland, Motril, and Nepal.

Now, sailing the irridescent seas,
they perch in the crow's nest on a wobbling gyre,
scanning horizons,
where chaos sings across the sky and hums
                          in every mountain, cloud, and wave.

And when they are certain of nothing,
they drop anchor and chart the ship,
or write a fish or nebula,
or name the Milky Way;
and then, like Moses, hold it up—their artifice,
a momentary order in the face of fate,
the fire from God's eyes forged,
their hallelujah—Here and Now.

Weighing anchor, making sail again,
they risk Bali and Barbados,
Sumatra, Kiruna, and Spain,
through foam, and crest, and trough,
through molecule and particle,
electron, neutron, quark,
and all the wondrous mysteries that mark their way.

Two Lives:

Making Supper at Lake George

In suspenders, white silk shirt, sleeves rolled, black bow tie,
Stieglitz cuts onions at the kitchen sink,
lays the purple skins on a cotton towel,
a tear runs into his mustache.
Setting the table, O'Keeffe carries plates and silver graciously,
            crooking her long fingers ostentatiously.
Her green muslin dress falls from one shoulder.
Her neck is strong.
She dreams of the sun-bleached skulls of horses.
He sees the dark pools of Dorothy's eyes.

A sudden gust and a boom of thunder
lift the lace curtain like a veil
and snuff the white candle on the table.
Alfred raises his eyes from the onions,
out the kitchen window, to the boiling sky.
Georgia looks up from placing a fork,
out the dining room window, across the yard;
            she sees the gray slate of the lake glazed at the base
            of the hills like the shining silver knife in her hand.
As the rain plops, a breath of ozone, wet wool,
and sweet grass
            sprays through the window screens.
Spring, the skin's thrill, breaks into goose bumps
on their bare arms
            and their nostrils swell with the fragrance of God.

The canvas edge of her calla lily
flutters like a hummingbird on the easel.
His cloud photos on the coffee table billow
and slide and rest again in disarray.
The book on the floor flips through many chapters.
A thin line of smoke streams from the candle.
In this light the wine is dark as blood in the two glasses
on the dining room table.

Georgia lifts her shoulders together
and her dress falls to the floor.
Alfred slips quickly and carefully from his clothes,
            draping them over a dining room chair.
She folds her easel and takes up her palette;
he fetches his camera from the coffee table,
                        and they walk into the rain,
                                    separately.
They do not look at each other for fear of bursting into flame.
The screen door bangs twice,
                    then taps
and murmurs on its hinges
in the storm.

Death at Camp Pahoka

"It is *choice* that decides which of the quantum worlds we measure
in our experiments, and therefore which one we inhabit."

John Gribbin

Kitchen crew,
rinse boy,
I dipped each plate
into the large stone sink of hot water
till garbage floated inches deep.
Under the surface
my hand seemed to slither
through intestines and the tails of dead rats.
One evening after mess,
nauseated by the steaming tubs of slime,
I staggered to my tent,
doubling over in the pine grove,
holding my gut until I collapsed on my cot.
The last I remember is the smell of tarp,
sweat trickling in the hair around my ears,
the whine of cicadas,
a centipede crawling across the shadows of leaves
that lay, scarcely moving, on the yellow canvas roof.

I'm sure I died that day
and woke into a different world,
a different kitchen,
where the kid who scraped the plates before I rinsed,
said he, like me, had never been away from home.
Though slop still filled the sink,
the pine grove stood more green and
stars more brilliant
above the Mess Hall.
          I wonder if an In Memoriam plaque
now hangs above that other sink—
"One more Boy Scout, First Class, Rinse Boy,
killed by swill."
But even more,
I wonder how I knew to choose this universe:
this charmed one,
this one with this daughter
to whom I pass each dish to dry,
who gives it to my son to put away
then snaps his butt with her towel,
this wife who wipes the table clean,
this life.

F. Richard Thomas was born in Evansville, Indiana. He attended Purdue University, University of Minnesota, and Indiana University. Currently, he is Professor of American Thought and Language at Michigan State University and editor/publisher of Years Press and *Centering* magazine. A sampling of his poems appear in *New Poems from the Third Coast* (Wayne State University Press). He has received a Michigan Council for the Arts award and two Fulbright Awards to teach in Denmark, as well as a recent grant from Michigan State University to complete an experimental novel, *First Communion: A Secular Catechism*. He lives with his wife Sharon, in East Lansing, Michigan, and spends part of every year in Las Cruces, New Mexico, where his son and daughter own and manage the Red Mountain Café.